RONNY ALLARD

THE UNDERTAKER DOWN UNDER

Ronny Allard
ronnyeallard@gmail.com
PO Box 9084, Harkaway Victoria 3806, Australia

First published in Australia 2020

Edited by Tanya Smith
Typeset by Nikki M Group
Cover design by Andrew Seymour

ISBN 978-0-645018-10-3 (print)
ISBN 978-0-645018-11-0 (ebook)

A catalogue record for this
book is available from the
National Library of Australia

Contents

About the Author

I immigrated to Australia in 1987 from Mauritius with my mum and my two siblings when I was only 7 years of age. I remember my mum trying to wake me from a deep sleep like I was late for school. I struggled to wake while noticing people shuffling out of the plane. It was then that I realised we had just landed, and while Mum was gathering all our belongings, all I wanted to do was get a few more minutes of sleep.

Throughout that year, I was thrown into a new world where I did not know the language and had to adapt to my new surroundings quickly. Little did I know that this would serve me well for the years to come, and prepare me for the future yet to arrive.

I moved to and from different schools and developed a knack for adapting to changes in my environment.

I was never really interested in school; I was the kid who required help in every class, given English was my second language. I felt I was always behind the eight ball but developed confidence in myself and I learnt to go with the flow. To this day, I'd say that adapting to any situation was the most important skill I acquired in my school years and it continues to serve me well.

Raised by a single mum, my siblings and I toed the line and never asked for anything. We moved to and from public housing for years before settling in a house Mum bought. By then, I was a young man working several part-time jobs. One of the many characteristics Mum bestowed on us was to work hard and appreciate what we have. Even though we didn't have much, Mum made us feel complete, and we always knew she loved us.

As a child with a bike in the 80s and 90s, exploring is what my best friend and I did. The school bell ringing at the end of the term to summon in the holidays was like the starting gun to a road trip – the road trip entailing riding around our neighbourhood looking for new adventures. Seeking new adventures was nothing new, and as time passed, we ventured further and further from home. Like many others who enjoyed the era of playing outside, the only *apple* we knew of back then was in the fruit bowl on the kitchen table.

Nothing in my childhood would indicate that I would first work as an undertaker and secondly, write a book about it. The most daring thing I remember doing as a kid was trying to beat my older brother at

2-square. For younger generations, this isn't an app on Google Play; it is a game played with a tennis ball on a rectangular-shaped 'court' divided into two boxes drawn on the ground, and using a hand for a racquet. We would play until one of us was tired of either losing or had had enough (that was usually me).

As the years went on, I met my wife at school, and we started dating. Even though we were high school sweethearts, we maintained our relationship after finishing school and today we are still together. We have four beautiful children, and my wife has always been by my side through thick and thin.

As a young man in school – not doing well – I knew school wasn't for me. I did what I had to do to pass, but started to worry about what I would do in the future. I played out the scenarios in my head of where I would end up one day. I knew I wasn't going to be a doctor or a lawyer, or anything that required good grades. And, not having anyone to push me in any one direction, the only job I knew that was hiring was as a storeman working full-time for a supermarket. So, I took that up. I then moved onto a job at a hardware store, working in the timber yard for four years. This was a job that opened my eyes to the different trades coming and going, but nothing prepared me for what was to come.

By this time, I had proposed to my girlfriend, soon to become my wife, and we had saved just enough for a deposit on our first home. We couldn't be happier. We were in our late teens and knew it was a bold step; however, it was the most logical step for us to move towards becoming adults and, more importantly, becoming independent.

Today, I am happy where I ended up. My worries didn't come to fruition. I've even taken up writing a few books. Never in a million years could I have imagined myself where I am today, and for that, I thank my wife for her support throughout my journey.

I decided to write about my experiences working as an undertaker, as the people I had shared my stories with loved hearing about the unusual cases I'd come across. While sharing these experiences in the stories to follow, I do not name names to protect the people involved. Also, please keep in mind that the stories I am about to share with you are my interpretation of what happened on the day, and the events leading up to my encounter with the deceased.

by Ronny Allard

Introduction

The year was 2001. I was in my early 20s and working in the timber yard of a large hardware store.

I distinctively remember three things about that year. Unfortunately, it was the year that two planes crashed into the World Trade Center. I watched on in disbelief like the rest of the world, trying to come to grips with what had just happened. Also that year, I bought my first road bike – a ZX 750 Kawasaki – the biggest bike I had ever jumped on. I was a bit intimidated, but the excitement of owning a sports bike surpassed all fears. I knew that if my mother discovered my intentions to purchase it, she would disapprove and try to talk me out of buying it – as I am sure most parents would. Today, I still enjoy riding bikes as much as I did all those years ago. When Mum finally found out, she exhibited some resistance as expected, but how can you talk sense to a young man with a brand-new motorcycle?

And the third thing that happened in 2001 was that I quit my job at the timber yard to become an undertaker. This wasn't just a random decision I decided one day, like wanting extra fries with an order after placing an order. Working in the timber yard, I had met all sorts of people and, it so happens, that one of the local funeral directors of a prestige funeral company and his employees regularly visited the hardware store, while doing ongoing renovations to the funeral house. I immediately struck a chord with them, and we had a chat every time they came in. Over time, I found out what they did for work. Their response wasn't what I expected as they did not come to the timber yard in a hearse, of course, and they were always dressed in casual work clothes. I was immediately intrigued. After some careful consideration, I worked up the courage to ask if they were hiring.

At first, and understandably, they were hesitant, with me being so young and with little to no life experience. They may have thought I wasn't ready to process what they endured daily. Looking back, I wouldn't blame them if this was what they thought. Their hesitation made me more resolute. The 'tell me I can't do something and I'll prove you wrong' attitude came into play. Their line of work to me seemed like a hidden, secretive organisation that only certain people could be a member. At the same time, my position at the timber yard was threatened and I was having issues with management. So, proactively, I phoned the director and said, 'Look, I'm happy to join your team. I'm not squeamish and I can handle myself pretty well. What do you say?'

'I'll think about it,' he responded at the time. However, the same day he said, 'Okay, we'll take you on board, but you understand what we do, right?'

'Sure!' I said, lying again. For one, I didn't know exactly what they did, and two, I didn't know how I would conduct myself around a dead body because I had never seen a dead body in my life. I'd seen dead birds and dogs and cats, so I figured, *how different could seeing a dead body really be?*

To me, taking a job with a funeral company was an adventure that I hadn't planned for – like going to a country and not knowing the language, and having just one suitcase and $20 in your pocket. There was no backing out now. So, this was the moment I was ripped from my comfort zone, with full knowledge that I was embarking on something unknown. It felt like I was taking a rocket to Mars.

The first day I arrived at the funeral home, I was nervous, to say the least. Pulling into the drive, I wondered to myself if I would last out the day, or maybe two, or possibly even a whole week. Little did I know I would spend approximately two years here. The comfort I took in that first walk from my car to the building was that I had already met most of these guys countless times and had joked around with them. What was new about this day, other than starting a new job, was that I had no idea what to expect – *I was like Alice walking down deep into the rabbit hole.*

As I push open the front door, I quickly scanned the area to take in the atmosphere. It felt like I was walking in on a funeral, but then I heard the chitter-chatter of talking and laughter. I made my way closer to the sound. As I entered the chapel, all heads turned to acknowledge my presence in a friendly manner.

'So, you're here,' someone quipped, 'I thought you'd never show up!' I had made sure I was on time, but this broke the ice. Comfortable conversation ensued and I quickly got a rundown on what to expect, and what to wear.

'Have you got a suit?' the main funeral director asked.

'Yes, I have my wedding suit,' I replied.

'Great! Wear that with some black shoes,' he responded.

The funeral director was a very likeable man; I'd say in his late thirties or mid-forties. He was an entrepreneurial type of guy; anything was within his grasp. He was very animated but stern. He was always up for a chat and you knew you couldn't bullshit this guy about anything; he was sharp.

He continued to explain what was involved and said who I would be working with. 'You'll get a text message with the details and have an hour to get to the site within your area. You'll take the body to a hospital to be certified that they are deceased and then take them, with the paperwork, to the coroner's office.'

After the rundown and some formalities, the guys and I did some maintenance around the funeral home. The two other employees were very friendly and, while working away, we shared some laughs and jokes. I felt at ease pretty quickly, but in the back of my mind, I was yearning for more information about what we were going to be doing exactly. I kept questioning myself – *have I made the right decision?*

All day, I put on a confident face, like I knew what I had signed up for. I remember the moment when I was asked casually by one of the other employees, 'Have you seen a dead body before?' *I mean what else do you get asked on your first day of work, right?*

I replied honestly, 'No! But I should be okay.' I was trying to sound casual as if I had just been asked if I wanted extra services at the dinner table.

This opened up the floodgates for the other guys to share stories of dead body encounters. To me, it felt like the exact moment I had leapt from the side of a cliff to jump in the water below, only to realise that my feet had left the security of the firm cliff side I was standing on previously. Now I was in freefall. As the stories came in, one at a time, it quickly turned into a competition of who attended what scene, with each story becoming more gruesome than the last. I knew I could walk away at any moment, but I was exactly where I'd been most of my life, finding comfort when I'm out of my depth.

By this stage, I may as well have jumped ship, taken the island and burnt my boat. It did cross my mind that they're probably trying to test me, to see if I had second thoughts, or if I would walk away. So, I listened carefully and took in some hints and advice they had for me. In the back of my mind, I was praying that I would never see half of the things they talked about – stories of decapitations, being threatened by a house full of drunks, suicides and the different ways people choose to take their own life. I don't know why I stayed, maybe because I didn't have another job to go to. I decided I may as well make the most of it.

A lot of the advice I was given was useful, like don't put your hand into the pocket of a person who had died from a drug overdose because there could be hidden needles (part of the job was to extract their possessions to hand over to the coroner). One piece of advice I wasn't prepared for was on how to combat the smell of rotting flesh. Someone suggested carrying Lynx Africa. Another suggested Vaseline under the nose. *I mean, who carries around Vaseline with them?* This quickly turned into a joke, and the laughter became more contagious.

By mid-morning, I felt at ease, like 1 was part of the gang. We went to the Subway next door for some lunch and waited for a call. Nothing came, so towards the end of the day, I headed home to wait. That night, I told my wife that I was more than ready to do whatever this job entailed. I now know that, at the time, I did not have the slightest clue of what I had signed up for.

The stories were one thing, but what I was about to experience was nothing short of anything I could have been prepared for.

In the chapters that follow is a collection of stories of what I encountered during my time as an undertaker, and the people whose lives crossed paths with mine, after they had died. I share with you an insight into what it's like to be an undertaker.

Welcome to my journey.

My First Encounter with a Deceased

*"The journey of a thousand miles
begins with one step."*
Lao Tzu

We are all born and then hopefully, if we're lucky, we live a peaceful life with people we love and people who love us. We experience everything in between and die surrounded by our loved ones.

Joe lived in the same neighbourhood all of his life. As a young man, he joined the army and saw the horrors of war. He came home, got married and stayed with his wife for life. They had a couple of children. Joe always played it safe and didn't like to take risks.

He lived a peaceful life, travelled the country with his wife, and was content with what he had. He never risked that life by trading on the stock market, buying an investment property or anything along those lines. He was satisfied with what he had. He paid his house off and tendered to his garden.

One day, Joe wakes up to find himself alone – his wife had passed away. He now lived in his quiet, orderly house, surrounded by memories of a life well-lived. There were some things he could not bring himself to throw away, even if he didn't know why his wife had bought them in the first place. Now, objects become more like a part of who she was. This brought him comfort when he glanced at them.

Joe's life now revolved around looking at his watch several times a day for no other reason than to check the time and to take countless pills. One day, Joe's body had taken its toll. He did exceptionally well to manage and fend for himself to a ripe old age. Anyone would be more than happy to reach the milestone Joe did.

THE SCENE

At approximately 6 p.m., my first call comes in that I've been anxiously waiting for. I received the name and the address as instructed. I knew my work colleague, who I was to be working with, would have also received the same text. She calls me to make sure I received the message and that I am getting ready. She says she'll be at my house in ten minutes. Sure enough, I was dressed in less than three minutes – like a firefighter heading to a house fire. I waited inside my front door, anxiously checking every 30 seconds to see if she had arrived. It felt like a lifetime. Then, like seeing a bus arrive, she pulled up by the front gate and tooted her horn.

I quickly called out my farewells and headed out the door like lightning. This was the start of my journey, a new chapter in life.

I jumped in the car with her – like a rally driver and the co-driver – and we started to head in the direction of the address we received. My first job was to locate the address in a street directory and find the quickest route. Back then, we were on the verge of GPS technology, but downloading an app on a Nokia 3310 was impossible – even to send a text, you would have to hit the '5' key three times to type the letter L! Phones were not as advanced as they are today.

On arrival at the address, it was difficult to make out the house from the street. The house was set back behind trees and overgrown bushes. By then, it was already becoming dark out, and the lack of street lights didn't help. Having been briefed in the car of what to expect and how to conduct myself in the presence of families and friends of the deceased, I tried to quickly remember what I had learnt before reaching the front door – a door representing the horrors I was dreadfully expecting. I think all of the butterflies brought a plus one to a party in the pit of my stomach, but I mustered up all the confidence I had. I acted like I was ready for *anything*.

The house inside had a distinctive, old, musty, damp smell about it. Immediately, I knew it wasn't a family who lived here, deducing that it was the residence of a singular, older person. We met with the police officers inside, who were the only people present. There were no family members and the paramedics, who were there earlier, had left when it was concluded that there was nothing that could be done to bring the deceased back to life.

After completing certain formalities with the police and filling out the required paperwork, my colleague and I proceeded to walk towards the bedroom. I swallowed the lump inside my throat as I entered the room of the deceased. There, lying in bed, was an elderly man. His hands were frozen in time, raised to his chest. To me, the cause of death seemed evident that he had died of a heart attack – an end he was powerless to prevent.

The other crew that we worked with had arrived on the scene. They moved in sync as they lifted the body of the lifeless man into a white sheet and onto a waiting trolley. I watched the procedure from the side, taking in as many details as I could. The deceased was wheeled out of his home. This would be the last time he moved along this hallway, past the walls where the dusty photographs of his life hung and out into the garden he had tended with loving hands – *never to return*. To witness this felt surreal and wondrous.

As I walked through the empty house, following the body, my mind switched to the life of the old man: *What kind of life has he lived? Where is his family? Had he been alone here for a long time? What was he like moments before his death?* It was at this point that I began to wonder how the decisions I had made in life had led me to this very moment.

After completing this job, I was thankful my first encounter wasn't anything like the guys had shared with me on my first day. I felt somewhat blessed it wasn't gruesome, and I wasn't thrown in the deep end. Even though it stayed with me for a long time to come, along with the questions it made me wonder, I was grateful to have made it through my first encounter with a deceased body without freaking out.

My next job was also an elderly man who had suffered a heart attack while driving. No one else was harmed, but the heart attack was fatal. From this moment onward, each time I had to strap my boots on, I knew what a privilege it was to spend those last moments with a fellow human being who had lived a life. Each encounter with a deceased body would intertwine its presence with my own life experiences and become my personal stories to share.

Joleen Joleen

"In his life there was only one woman.
The other one."
Ljupka Cvetanova

At Sue's 30th birthday party, Jeff was a plus one of a friend and Sharon was Sue's best friend. When Jeff and Sharon met, they were automatically drawn to each other. Not long after, they were an item. Sometime later, Jeff and Sharon married with Sue as the maid of honour. Their wedding was memorable, to say the least.

Jeff and Sharon lived a pretty ordinary life for the next 20 years. Each having children from previous marriages, by this time, the children had all but moved out. Jeff worked in construction most of his adult life, and long hours were part of the job. Lately, however, Jeff had been working longer hours than usual, starting earlier and earlier; not every day but some days, and some weeks it was almost every other day.

Sharon stayed in touch with Sue, and they would usually catch up for coffee twice a week and chat about all of life's issues, and share the latest gossip. Sue now lived on her own, a short drive away. She had married and had two daughters, but the marriage had not worked out, and her husband had left. After the divorce proceedings, Sue lived in the family home and raised her daughters. Now, the daughters had grown up and moved out, and Sue lived in the house alone. She worked part-time at a florist and sought comfort and companionship in Sharon at their regular catch-ups.

Over numerous cups of coffee, Sharon would ask Sue if she had found the man to fulfil her life. To Sharon, Sue was too attractive to stay single. Sue would always say the same thing when asked: all the good men are either married or gay, I have tried dating sites, all the men my age either want a caretaker or a mother figure, the men I meet are just too needy – she was done raising kids. As far as Sue was concerned, or so Sharon thought, she was content living on her own; she didn't need a man in her life to be happy.

THE SCENE

Early one morning, I was fast asleep when I was awoken by the dreaded text message tone of my phone – two loud, distinctive beeps from my Nokia. I leant over to check who it was from, and, if it was from a colleague, hoping it was a false alarm. *God, did I hope it was at times, especially at 4 a.m.!* Sure enough, it was another job. I had been out the night before, so I felt it was way too early for people to die, however in my books, I had become apt at quickly getting up, dressed and in the car that pulled up on cue not long after the text message was received.

So, I suited up military-style, looking like one of the *Men in Black*, with my white shirt and black tie, and black suit with black shoes to match. Although I looked smart, I was feeling like Sleepy from *Snow White and the Seven Dwarfs*. When the fresh air outside hit my skin, I had wished I had chucked a jacket on. I hoped the near approaching dawn would warm the air. I got into the driver's seat of a warm car with the heater blaring.

The address was a short, 15-minute drive from home. We slowly pulled up at the house. An attending police officer noticed our arrival, exited the house and made her way to my driver-side window. I lowered the window and was greeted by a young policewoman. She spoke to my partner and I in a concerned tone. 'Hi. Before you go in, one thing you should know …'

'Okay,' I said, 'what's that?' Now, from this moment, she had my full attention. I had never been given a pep talk at the car before entering a scene. My partner and I knew something was serious. My heart rate automatically increased. There was excitement in not knowing what I was about to hear.

'When you come in, pick up the body in the room on the right and say nothing.' She went on. 'Don't even talk to the family, just grab him and leave.'

I responded with a worried, unsettling tone. 'Sure.' I was thinking to myself: *What the hell has happened here that we don't know?*

We got out of the car and followed the police officer to the front door. We were a couple of metres behind her when I asked in a soft voice with tremendous curiosity. 'So, who are we picking up?' I tried to sound casual, but I could hear the fear in my voice; I was expecting the worst.

My question was met with no reply. Maybe she didn't hear me. I asked again in a subtle but louder tone.

'Umm, so what's happened?' Again, no reply. I know she had heard me the second time. The silence became somewhat uncomfortable, and was followed immediately with a deep gut-turning thought: *What on Earth are we about to witness here?*

It was a short walk from the car, across the front lawn, to the house. As we approached, my mind filled with horrifying thoughts of what I was about to witness: *Is this the scene of a multiple murder? Are children involved? Is this going to be on the National News later and have the nation gasping?* All of these thoughts were running through my mind, while my head was screaming, '*I'm not ready for this!*' I quickly pulled myself together. I knew the butterflies in my stomach had flown away long ago. I reminded myself that I'm here to do a job – this is my job. I just have to deal with whatever I see and do what is required of me.

I took a deep breath and the front door swung open. By this point, I was psyching myself up, not knowing what awaited behind door number 1, like a contestant on *Fear Factor*. Standing behind the police officer, I walked inside. A single, soft, dim glow from under a lampshade illuminated the corridor. As the police woman stepped to one side, I could see a single light hovering above a small, round, wooden kitchen table, and a mother in her early fifties was being comforted by her two daughters, in their early to mid-twenties. They were sitting at the table with distressed and concerned looks on their faces, yet not one of them was crying. I found this odd. Most scenes I had attended where loved ones were present, people were crying, as expected. Families had every reason to be in the state they were – we weren't delivering pizza. This family, however, were acting differently – it wasn't the reaction I was used to.

As I looked to my right into the master bedroom, I could see the deceased – a man in his late forties or early fifties, with a medium build, and not an ounce of fat on him, lying in bed, stark naked. He looked fit for his age like he looked after himself – the sought of guy you would think less likely to die from a heart attack. Yet, there he was. He had exited the world the same way he had come into it – not a single piece of clothing on him; however, he wasn't quite the way he was when he entered the world … To address the elephant in the room, it was clear that this man was having the time of his life when he died! He still carried an erection from his last breath. It was hard not to notice he packed a full package – this thing looked like a weapon of mass destruction! And, there it was for all to see.

At this point, my mood had changed from fearing the unexpected to a more relaxed and sombre tone, knowing my worst nightmare hadn't come to fruition. We approached the man and wrapped him in a white sheet. We picked him up and placed him on the stretcher that was waiting in the corridor by the front door. We were within eyesight of the women at the end of the corridor, who were watching our every move. I was still confused as to why no crying or distress was coming from any of the women. I would say this was somewhat unsettling. Things just didn't seem to make sense; one minute he's making love and the next, he dies, and his family isn't one bit sorry for their loss?

A standard practice we do, as a common courtesy before we leave with the deceased, is to give a business card to the next of kin. This directs them to the funeral director and councillors they can contact during business hours. When we get a call-out to a scene, the people at the address often have many questions, and in many cases, this is the first time they have had to deal intimately with the passing of a friend or a loved one. The card provides the main contact for them, who can direct them to the services they will require to make funeral arrangements and insurance claims, and so forth.

Just as I pulled the white business card out of my top pocket, and started to head over to the family, the same police officer, who had greeted us at the car earlier, interjects. She grabbed hold of my arm with a firm grip, as if I had just been pulled over for an offence, and says in a quiet, firm tone so only we could hear. 'Don't talk to the family! This isn't his house. We're trying to contact his wife and let her know that her husband has died.'

'Oh, okay!' I reply with a confused look on my face.

The officer continues. 'This is his wife's best friend's house.'

"OHH!" was the only word that I could find in my vocabulary at the time to reply. No further explanation was required. Now, I fully understood what had happened here! I didn't know whether to be embarrassed for the guy, his wife, or the friend. I was just glad I wasn't in any part of this scenario come sunrise.

Once outside, the young police officer explained that the man would leave early for work, telling his wife he needed to start earlier than expected. He would then go and pay her best friend a visit before heading off to work at the usual time, while his wife was asleep.

After leaving the premises, I don't know what happened. I will leave that to your imagination as to how the day played out for all parties involved. I would think that the death of a loved one in the arms of an unknown – but in this case known – love is news no one would want to hear … perhaps a cautionary warning to those who *play on the sidelines*.

Peace Train

"Sometimes, even to live is an act of courage."
Lucius Annaeus Seneca

Max loved his job. He was surrounded by friends and family and had a happy marriage. Looking in from the outside, he had everything anyone would love to have, even down to his bubbly personality that would light up any room. In fact, at parties, he would be the one making everyone laugh.

What only a few people knew about Max was that, while he was busy making everyone laugh and have a good time, Max himself felt like he was alone in this world. For years, he had suffered from depression. Looking at him, you wouldn't notice. Max had seen countless shrinks and tried just about everything to shake the dark thoughts in his mind. His marriage had always endured this battle – his wife understood this –

but at times, she felt that there was only so much she could take. Nonetheless, she stood by him.

One day, while at work, Max overheard that the steel manufacturing plant (where he worked) could possibly lose a significant contract and the bosses upstairs were doing everything to salvage the deal. Thinking management had it under control, he didn't think much of it. A couple of days later, on a Friday afternoon, some of the workers were called into the manager's office one by one. As they walked out, they informed their co-workers that they had taken a severance package and would move on. As the afternoon went on, Max thought he might have avoided the sack when one of the managers called Max on the in-house phone and asked him to pop in. Max's body changed immediately. He knew this feeling – the anxiety of not knowing what was to come. He felt warm. His hands started to shake. His legs even felt uncomfortable standing up. He knew the news he was about to hear was not going to be good. Max walked into the office and saw Dan and John, the directors, sitting on chairs facing the door. Max sat on the vacant chair, which was positioned to face the two.

John jumped straight to the point. 'So, you've probably heard of what's been happening,' he began. Max moved uncomfortably in his seat.

'Yes, I have,' he replied, trying to hide the nervous tone in his voice. 'Do I still have a job?'

'About that,' Dan interjected. 'You've been with us for about five years now, and we appreciate all the effort you have put into this company …'

'So, I'm getting fired?' Max questions, cutting Dan off abruptly.

'It's not easy to do, and we value you and the others highly, but yes, we have to let a few people go,' Dan finishes off what he was saying.

'So, what does that mean for me now?' Max asked, directing his puzzled gaze at both men.

'You have about eight weeks of holiday leave that you can cash in but, as far as that, there isn't much more we can offer because you've only been here five years,' John replied.

'Right.' Max looked at the ground and gave a defeated sigh. He mustered the energy to rise from the chair and thank the men. He walked out, passing his co-workers without saying a word. He headed to the locker room, collected his stuff and walked out of there for the last time. Arriving at his car, he chucked his things on the back seat and placed himself behind the driver's wheel.

And, there he sat, staring straight ahead.

His mind was unsettled. The darkness he knew well was clouding his every thought. *I'm a failure. What can I do now? Nobody will want me. I won't find another job.*

Max had recently turned 50. His body wasn't as fit as a 30-year-old. His skills were limited from five years working on the assembly line. He couldn't help but think of all the negativity in his life and how this would affect him and his wife financially. Finally, he started the car. The drive home was slow; he dreaded seeing his wife's face, hearing her voice, and witnessing the look of disappointment and stress in her eyes when he broke the news.

He pulled the car into the driveway and turned off the engine. He took a deep breath as he entered the house. Immediately, though, he lost all courage and decided not to tell his wife just yet. *When the time is right,* he thought.

'Hi,' he said as he entered the kitchen where his wife was preparing dinner.

'What's the matter?' she asked, knowingly. She knew him well, knew his moods, and could sense when something was up.

This caught Max off guard. He was never a good liar. 'Nothing,' he lied and headed straight to the lounge room. *Maybe some TV will settle my nerves.* He picked up the remote control and began flicking through the channels, hoping to find something remotely interesting. No such luck. After scanning through all of the channels about three times, he decided that that too was useless in taking his mind of what had just happened. He felt more of a failure than ever; that he couldn't live up to a man who could provide for his wife. He tried to shake the lingering feeling that this was the end – that he would never find another job, that they would lose the house, that his wife would leave him for someone more worthy of her love …

Max got up and grabbed his keys from the kitchen bench, where he had left them only minutes earlier.

'Where are you heading off to in such a hurry?' his wife asked.

Max avoided her gaze and lied for a second time. 'Goin' to the Sports Bar for a drink with the guys. Back soon.'

She replies, 'Okay, have fun. Don't be long.'

Max walked to his car, knowing full well that he may not be *back soon*. A dark thought told him that he probably would never be back, never hold his wife again, never look at her lovely smile. *She deserves better,* he thought. And, with that, he reversed out of the driveway for the last time.

Max drove around in a blur. Dark clouds blinded his every thought, circling around and around in his head. Every scenario, every scene, every outcome, every word was stuck in the dark clouds. He pulled up at the local train station. He sat in his car, alone, and waited for the afternoon train, packed with commuters, to reach the station before deciding his fate.

THE SCENE

One afternoon, a text came through with an address just one block away from where I was. I looked at the message with some confusion as it read 'train station', as opposed to the usual house address or intersection. *That's weird,* I thought. I got ready, and we headed to the train station. It was evident from the text that someone had jumped in front of a train, but it became more evident as we pulled up. The main road was blocked off, with police officers directing traffic away from the station. We had to weave the van between the traffic and roadblocks before pulling up at the scene. As we walked onto the station platform, we knew straight away that someone had jumped in front of a train a short distance from the platform. This was the first train accident I had attended. I thought I knew what to expect as I had listened to the other guys talk of their experiences. They had mentioned that it is a job that can take a while, as you have to walk a hundred metres up and down the tracks to make sure every part of the deceased body is retrieved – big and small. The stories had painted a pretty gruesome picture, but it was nothing to witnessing the carnage myself. Again, the excitement built in my body as I was about to experience another first firsthand – with my hands literally.

We were met by a scene of police officers and emergency services, on the platform and then down on the train tracks. As always, I tried to act professional, although in the back of my mind I thought, *only a couple of years ago I was coming home from school about this time, and now I'm working alongside emergency services to dive into this carnage.* To say I wasn't scared would be a lie. I tried to visualise the gruesome scenes from the stories I had been told to brace myself for what I might encounter, so that there would be no surprises. However, just as much as you might try to prepare yourself for a horror film, you can never be totally prepared for what is to come.

Deliberately or not, a person is now scattered and strewn across the tracks. It's not a sight I would wish upon anyone to see. Nevertheless, people gathered as close as they could to view the incident from a distance. From where I was standing, directly over the body parts, I don't think there would have been many people wanting to see what I saw. And it was our job to make sure every bit was collected.

We approached the attending officers at the scene and were briefed on the cause of death and the relevant details leading up to the impact. Even though I could see what had happened, being told what had happened was still a shock. It made me think of why anyone would want to take their life in this way. I pictured in my mind what the final moments would have been like, I just couldn't believe what had just happened. My mind was like a constantly working *Rubik's Cube* – twisting and matching and rematching and twisting some more. I was trying to find the right combination to make sense of what my brain was trying to process every moment I was there.

As the late afternoon dawned upon us, the last train pulled into the station, terminating earlier than expected. This was now the end of the line, and no more trains would pass before our job and that of the investigators was complete. The last commuters shuffled away, heading home after a long day to their families. Our job was just beginning. We placed the trolley as close as possible to the side of the tracks where the main part of the torso lay. This was not a clean and clear operation, to state the obvious.

As we began this gruesome task, I noticed how the body parts could reveal how the event unfolded. I could see exactly where he had jumped from as that is where the entrails began. He was then struck by the front of an eighty-tonne train full of passengers. This knocked the man backwards with considerable force onto his back and dragged him about fifty metres across the sharp, jagged corners of the railway ballast rocks. His back was ripped open like a sardine can and his organs and spine were strewn across the tracks, as his body tumbled like being stuck in a washing machine. These parts now resembled rose petals scattered along the aisles created by the parallel train tracks.

We walked over to the torso, which had only one leg and one arm attached. Fingers were missing. We attempted to pick the torso up to place it on the prepared white sheet. This didn't go to plan. Because every bone in his body was broken, the best way to describe what we were tackling would be to compare the torso to a giant, gelatinous rucksack filled with sticks and thick jelly. We endeavoured with the help of the attending emergency workers and the police to finally get the sloppy, giant water balloon with no grips to grip onto, into the white sheet and onto the trolley.

Never having attended a train accident before, or even having seen one in my life, this was very confronting and uneasy. This feeling quickly turned to frustration as I made my way along the tracks and tried to grip onto body parts which would slip out of my hands. We were wearing gloves to protect ourselves, but it didn't take away the feeling of the texture: squishy, hard, soft, rubbery, waxy, sharp, smooth …

We quickly worked away, walking up and down the tracks with oversized zip-lock bags and clear freezer bags. We filled these bags with everything from fingers and toes to a foot, organs, fatty bits – anything that was big enough to pick up. I couldn't tell you how many bags we used – it was too many to count, but we did our best to find every bit.

As sunlight was fading by the minute, we had to try and use the little daylight still shining over the horizon to our advantage. We could feel the eyes of the residents, whose houses backed onto the train tracks, peeping through and over their back fences, curious to see what was happening and how bad it was. Subsequently, the temperature began to cool. This caused the body parts scattered along the railway lines to steam up as the body hadn't had much time to cool. This can happen due to a combination of the time of day and the speed in which we reach an accident site. I don't think anyone expects this to happen when the temperature changes so quickly.

At one point, I came across the man's heart laying on the tracks, like it was surgically and neatly removed and placed gently in that one particular spot by a surgeon. I took a moment to double-check that it was the heart. The reality set in at that moment, that just an hour prior, this man had life as blood travelled through this beating heart. Yet, here it sat – dormant. I had never seen a human heart before, but there was no mistaking its identity: the perfectly-formed, slightly asymmetric shape, the colour, the aorta.

I paused for a moment and, with awe, fixated my eyes on the lifeless organ I was now holding in my right hand. Uninhabited now by the blood that so recently flowed in and pumped out, I was unable to break the hypnotic gaze. *The crucial organ for life was resting in the palm of my hand.* The sound of a police officer's voice broke my gaze. As I turned my head to the side, I saw one of the officers staring directly at the heart with the same look I had on my face. I overheard him say to his partner, who was standing beside him, 'LOOK! That's his heart.' He then reached for his flashlight on his hip and shone a beam of light directly on me. They shared my sense of awe. I turned slightly to my left and extended my arm a little to give them a better view.

I had paused for probably about 3 seconds, yet it seemed like so much longer. With heat radiating off the heart and generating steam, still warm in my hand, I placed it carefully in a clear plastic zip-lock bag. It felt surreal, while at the same time feeling fragile and vulnerable – that one small organ beats an entire lifetime to keep us alive.

I continued collecting. Just as I was about to wrap up, I heard a police officer yell out that a body part was stuck between the tracks at the road crossing. As I walked over to investigate, with a bag in hand, I saw a couple of emergency workers and my colleague trying to unwedge something from between the steel track and the road. The emergency workers stood aside to let me have a closer look. I could see a long chunk of meat wedged under the steel. My partner and I pulled at the eye fillet-looking flesh and managed to free most of it, but there was some resistance from the last piece. It wasn't breaking free, no matter how hard we tugged. I soon realised that the bony pieces that were stuck were his knee, and the flesh we had managed to pull free was his thigh muscle. We tugged and pulled on the remaining ligament to free his kneecap. The best way to describe the situation would be like pulling a glass free from inside another glass that had been neatly jammed, and trying not to break the glasses in the process. A police officer asked if we had a crowbar. We didn't. Then someone suggested using the end of a flashlight, but the butt of the flashlight was too big to get between the track and the tar.

Time wasn't on our side. We needed to clear this area as quickly as possible, and we couldn't leave the kneecap behind for the public to see or animals to feed off. It became more and more evident that if we were to free this kneecap from the tracks, it would have to be broken into two parts. It was then that one of the attending emergency workers suggested using a jagged rock. A rock was not hard to find. Someone picked one up from the side of the tracks and managed to knock the kneecap free – it was as simple as that. It wasn't the ideal tool, but it worked. It was a horrible sight to witness, but it worked.

Soon after, we loaded the trolley with all the bags and the main torso into the van and did a double-check that we hadn't missed anything. We then proceeded to the nearest hospital to certify the body before heading to the coroner's office.

As we completed the job and drove towards home, I had a weird sense of accomplishment. I felt uneasy with this feeling as I didn't want to take any satisfaction at the expense of a man's life. I had listened to the stories about train accidents from the other guys – now I had my own story to tell. I now knew what to expect if I received another call to a train accident. That doesn't mean I would be any more at ease. I was fortunate, though, as I did not have to attend another accident involving a train again.

That evening, I headed to bed not long after arriving home. As I began to fall asleep, I suffered from hypnogogic jerks each time I started to drift off to sleep. Hypnogogic jerks, also known as hypnic jerks, are brief, sharp and sudden contractions of the body just as you're about to fall asleep. They can also occur when you're startled and scared and can be linked to anxious thoughts and stress. Even though I felt relaxed and calm, my brain hadn't had the time to process the situation, and thus it was still actively sending out all sorts of signals. This isn't a serious condition to have; its just a phenomenon that occurs. After the day I had, I wasn't surprise when it happened. A short while later, I was able to fall into a deep sleep.

The most common question I get asked is: *How could you do a job like that and for it not to affect you?* I would say I am lucky. I have never suffered from depression or had any mental issues relating to the work I did. People mentally and physically react differently to stress. Some are better equipped to handle stressful situations than others. I guess I could rationalise what I had witnessed in my own way. I don't think it has affected me to this day and that may be due to always having to adjust to a new situation as a young kid. I can appreciate the advantages of being placed in different situations now and being able to fit in like an old glove.

Only the Lonely

"In life, periods of solitude were blessings.
Dying alone was a bitter curse."
FAYE KELLERMAN

Matilda was born shortly after the First World War and lived through the Second World War. She was self-sufficient; never one to ask for help. After her husband died, a dog was always by her side for companionship.

Of late, she'd had a few health scares but nothing too serious. She had always eaten well and enjoyed her morning walks for years until her hips started to give her grief. Matilda was the woman everyone in the neighbourhood knew, and she knew everyone. She would know which flowers were in season and, over the years, was the proud owner and maker of one of the best rose gardens in the area. Matilda liked to sprinkle bird seed near her front doorstep and watch the variety of birds that came to eat there. Sometimes, she would even buy very little for herself so that she had enough money to buy treats for her pets.

Matilda watched the kids in the neighbourhood grow up to become adults themselves. As time passed like sand through the hourglass, children stopped playing outside. Neighbours moved out while new people moved in. A couple of the houses were turned into units. Her neighbourhood, which was once bustling with the screams and laughter of neighbourhood children running around and riding their bicycles before dark, now stood silent apart from the occasional arriving or departing car.

Matilda grew accustomed to her ever-changing surrounds. As long as she had a companion by her side, she was content. Sometimes, the Red Cross would come and visit her, but the visits were few and far between now. She was still able to drive herself to the local shops and her doctor appointments, but she had begun to notice that even that was becoming more difficult. One night, after watching her favourite TV shows for one last time, she went off to bed.

THE SCENE

It was mid-afternoon when we received a call to an address on the outskirts of the city suburbs. We arrived at an old, dilapidated house. It looked like the owner last tendered to the garden in the summer three years prior. It was evident that some maintenance was required to the house, along with some tender loving care. As we arrived, there were a few police vehicles parked on the front lawn, wherever they could fit. Some officers were casually walking in and out of the house. Sometimes, when turning up to a scene, it isn't hard to find the house we are looking for. That was the case this time.

We made our way inside through the secured, old flyscreen door that was barely hanging on its hinges. As we entered the foyer, we were directed along the hallway to the kitchen. The kitchen was an average looking, old-style room that looked like it had hosted many Sunday roasts among friends. There were papers and documents scattered over the kitchen table and bench. Police officers were moving in and around in a seemingly organised chaos, but we managed to find the main police attendee to fill out our part of the paperwork. He gave us a rundown of the situation. He informed us that an elderly woman had died approximately three months ago and her body was in the bedroom on the floor. After the quick explanation, he directed us to the near bedroom, where the body lay.

This was to be my first decomposed body. I was somewhat excited in a way to see what I was about to see. Thinking back to the stories the guys had shared with me on my first day, I had never forgotten the one where a body had not been discovered for about a year. Apparently, it had mummified under the conditions. *Was that what I was about to witness?* Images of touring through Egyptian burial tombs and pyramids crossed my mind, but what I was about to see was nothing like a holiday.

Arriving at the bedroom door, I slowly but carefully pushed it open to reveal a distinctive but subtle smell of rotting flesh. It was very dark, so I reached to flick the light on. Finding the switch, to my dismay, the light didn't turn on. A voice from behind informs, 'there's no electricity. It's been cut off.' *That would explain why the only light in the house was the little that shone through the open curtains in the living room.* After a few moments, my eyes adjusted to the darkness, and we entered the room. I could start to make out some objects in the dimly lit room. I noticed an old but slight woman sitting by the side of her bed on the floor. She was in a resting position like she was sleeping peacefully amongst the commotion going on around her. Draped over her lifeless body was a colourful, knitted blanket as if to keep her warm when she was alive.

As I stepped closer and settled my gaze upon the lady's face, I stopped in my tracks. I blinked a few times in case my eyes were playing tricks on me in the darkness, before taking a second look. I looked her directly in the eye, and again, she winked at me, as if she was trying to open her eyes. Now, at this moment, if I were alone, I would have run for the hills – I've seen enough scary movies to know what happens next! But, having the support of the officers and my colleague beside me, I summoned up the courage to lean over and have a proper look. I didn't want to sound foolish by saying anything about the possibility that this woman may be alive unless I was absolutely sure. I could only imagine the headlines; *Undertaker finds dead woman alive!* As I looked closer into her eyes, I realised she wasn't winking at me at all, to my relief. It was a swarm of maggots that had eaten her eyeballs and were wriggling inside her eye sockets. They were still feasting on what was left, making their way over one another as the glimmer of light flicked off them to form the perfect illusion of an eye from a short distance.

As disgusting as the swarm of maggots were, I suddenly felt normal again, and exhaled. Everything fell into perspective. It was like finally knowing the answer to a riddle. I'm glad I didn't succumb to my basic instinct and shout out, 'She's alive!' Everyone would have had a good laugh though, at my expense.

I stepped over the woman's body as it was the only path to get to the other side of her, while my partner was positioned on the other side. I grabbed the blanket with one hand and pulled it away to the side. In doing so, I unveiled a foul, gigantic, wriggling pile of maggots. They were all over her body. It was like opening Pandora's box – maggots dead and alive. I heard the mutters of disgust at the sight echo through the room by those who witnessed the display.

This also unveiled the heavy putrid smell of the maggots, which had been lying there for months undisturbed, and the rotting flesh. This was a hundred times worse than speaking to someone with morning breath. Straight away, I thought of all the advice given to us to combat the smells we might come across. No one had ever said dynamite, but that's the only thing that would have worked this time. The smell was enough to make you throw up. The only thing we could do was to run out of the room as quickly as we could to get some valuable fresh air.

Of course, we had to go back into the room, though all the police personnel at this time were outside. A few came back into the house, but no one was brave enough to walk back into the bedroom. Each time I went in, I held my breath for as long as I could, remembering the times at the swimming pool as a kid that I could go about thirty seconds before I needed air. Well thirty seconds is not long at all! We took another deep breath and entered the room for the last time to lift her lightweight body and her clothing onto the trolley.

What I wasn't expecting was just how light her body was. It was like lifting a shopping bag out of the trolley. All the blood and fat were all but eaten away by the maggots; the only thing left was her mummified skin and bones. We strapped her to the trolley and wheeled her out.

It was the time of year where we were coming out of winter, meaning she must have died in late autumn. With the fluctuation in temperature from cold to warm and back to cold again, her body was able to go unnoticed by the neighbours for a few months. The cold weather prevented her body from rapidly decomposing, and as the temperature began to warm up leading into spring, the smell would have permeated the air. This, in turn, led the foul odour to drift into the neighbouring houses. The police were called to investigate and discovered her body.

While finishing up, sadly a police officer asked, 'What do we do about the dog?'

What dog? One of the officers opened the door to the spare room, and my heart sank to the pit of my stomach. There, on the floor just inside the door, lay a poodle-like dog on its side. You could have mistaken it for a sleeping dog, but it was evident that the dog was no longer alive.

The saddest part of this discovery was that on the morning after the lady died, the dog had no one to release it from what would become its tomb – stuck there barking till it died. Someone said to call the vet. We left with the lady but drove away leaving her beloved companion behind. It was sad to think that no one heard or came to see why the dog was barking or to check in on the old lady after so many days.

Hey Brother

"A million words would not bring you back,
I know because I tried ... neither would
a million tears, I know because I cried."
AUTHOR UNKNOWN

Jim's dad was a minister. Living by strict rules all of his life was something Jim hated. Then, Jim and Julie met at bible study. They formed a strong bond and started to see each other every day.

After Jim's father found out about the relationship, he wasn't too pleased, but not long after, Jim and Julie decided to marry and moved into a rental house together. Jim got a job on a construction site, which paid well enough to enjoy a good life. He mixed with some friends who introduced him to cocaine. Each week, the guys would go out for drinks. Amid the drinks, they would do cocaine, and each week, they would take turns shouting a round of cocaine. This became a weekly habit.

Soon, Jim's cocaine habit became more than once a week with friends and he began to bring some home.

Julie and Jim always smoked the occasional weed to chill out after a long week, but feeling audacious, cocaine began to creep more and more into their lives.

Always living a clean life as the son of a preacher man, Jim's life had now strayed far from its humble beginnings. This apple could not have fallen further from the tree. More and more of Jim's and Julie's pay was devoted to their expensive drug habit.

As the years passed by, the life Jim and Julie dreamed of all but vanished. Now, with two kids to look after, they were living on handouts and donations just to get by. The kids wore worn clothes and barely had food in their lunchboxes for school. One day, Jim's frustrations of not succeeding like a lot of his friends – who had given up their drug use and changed their lives for the better – turned to anger and he took a swing at Julie. It knocked her to the ground and on her way down, she knocked their son over, resulting in a split lip and a black eye.

The next day at school, one of the teachers noticed the boy's injuries and immediately reported it to Human Services. Human Services arrived the next day at their home to find Julie in a comatose state, high on drugs. She was laying on the rubbish covered sofa with last night's dinner still on the coffee table amongst the empty wrappers.

Just then, Jim arrived home and walked in demanding what was going on. As they tried to address him, he became violent and started shouting. Human Services called the police, and an ambulance was called for Julie. It was evident that the children were not living in an environment needed for a healthy childhood. They were placed in foster care that same night, and Jim was arrested after finding drugs on the premises.

Julie was ordered into rehab, while Jim was sentenced to attend anger management classes if they were to see their kids again. Two years later, Jim and Julie were in the process of trying to get their kids back. One evening, they were subjected to a surprise drug test as part of the conditions to regain custody. Both Jim and Julie failed the drug test; according to the test levels, they were as high as they were when they first got tested. The children would remain in foster care.

Two months after they failed their test, and not knowing where their children were living, they received a phone call from Human Services. Julie answered the phone. The only word she was able to say was, 'Hello'. After that, she stayed silent, listening. Jim knew something was wrong. As Julie's eyes began to swell with tears and lips began to tremble, Jim rushed to the phone as Julie collapsed to the ground crying uncontrollably. Jim picked up the phone to hear the words, 'We are truly sorry.' Jim threw the handpiece against the wall and then wrapped his arms around Julie, fearing the worst.

Sometimes, I look back on my childhood and wonder what it would have been like having a father-figure in my life. Not getting what you want is sometimes a wonderful stroke of luck, according to the Dalai Lama.

The story I am about to share with you probably hit closer to home for me than any other job I attended. My siblings and I grew up in housing commission houses. We knew what it was like to stretch a dollar, like many others who know what I'm talking about. My mother was a single mum for as long as I can remember – I knew the struggles she faced. I also know how cruel kids can be.

There's a theory I heard from a good friend of mine who has known me since I was a pimply-faced kid. He said that sometimes bad things happen, but it depends on who we are and how we deal with gut-blowing situations that change our lives. Some people are defeated and spend a lifetime recovering from the blows life hands out, and others are galvanised by the blows life delivers. They get back up – blow after blow – no matter how hard life hits them, and start over again. I agree, but I also believe we all have our limits, and at some point, we might reach it.

THE SCENE

The most painful goodbyes are the ones that are never said and never explained.

One afternoon, about 4 p.m., a text message came through for a job located in a town called Rosebud. Rosebud was named after a shipwreck in the early 1900s where the locals stripped the ship for building materials – the name stuck. The town is a popular tourist destination along the beaches. We didn't mind the drive at all – approximately forty-minutes weaving through small, scenic towns and over rolling hills. Plus, the long drive gave us time to talk.

Still midway through our usual small talk, we realised we had arrived at our destination. We pulled up at the address and got out of the car. We walked to the front door, with our pads in one hand, like we had done a million times before.

As we were about to reach the front door, like many other doors before, the door flings open to our surprise, revealing a police officer behind the door. He had been waiting for our arrival. Not having to guess, we knew something serious had happened, more so than usual. It must have been something about his manner. He walked outside and greeted us with a profound sadness looming behind his face that was only visible through his defeated eyes. He gave us a rundown of what we were dealing with, carefully selecting his words. I was taken back by how devastated the police officer was while telling us what had happened, as if he was delivering bad news about someone we loved. Whatever the feeling was walking up to the door, in a split second, it was completely changed to a sense of sorrow.

'The deceased is a young boy in his early teens. He's inside the back shed,' he tells us.

I could tell that having to mutter those words was not easy for him. We go to see if there is access to get a trolley close to the back shed and identify any obstacle we might encounter along the way. As we pushed the trolley towards the shed, I wasn't looking forward to what I was about to see.

A few kids were standing by and around the shed, who may have lived at the house. They stood aside to make way for us to walk in a single file. I stepped inside a dark, barren shed. To my sorrow, I see a lifeless young boy balancing by a rope around his neck, arms flopped by his side. The tips of his toes were touching the ground, stopping him from spinning.

For a moment, I stared in disbelief. We've encountered people much older who had taken their life but never someone so young. He would have been no more than ten years younger than I was. He was the youngest deceased person I'd seen so far. I couldn't understand why he did what he did. He looked like any ordinary kid I would have passed by at school not too long ago. It killed my soul to see him hanging there.

We began to bring him down by cutting the rope and lowering his body onto the ground. One thing we're taught to do with someone who has hanged themselves is not to undo the knot. We are instructed to cut the rope anywhere along the straight piece and to turn over the knot to the coroner. It's not every time that people use rope. We've encountered belts, hose, wire and whatever is at hand, so we make sure we carry a serrated knife to cut through most materials.

When the knot is handed into the coroner's office, the coroner will examine the knot and be able to tell if it's been tied by a right or left-handed person, and what sort of training the person, if any, would have had if it is a specialised knot. The coroner's office would have to determine if the person did commit suicide or if the death was staged. For the same reason, they would take a blood sample from a person after death who was found to have gassed themselves in a car. This is to measure the level of oxygen and carbon monoxide from the car exhaust, to determine if the person was killed before entering the car or afterwards. These were some interesting facts that we became aware of.

After we placed the body of the boy on the trolley and wrapped him in a white blanket, we made our way to the car and loaded the stretcher before shutting the rear doors. Before we left, I asked the police officers, 'Who do we provide our card with the details to?' We had not seen the parents, only a few young boys who were at the back shed.

A police officer responded, 'The sister is inside the house – you can give her the card'.

Trying not to look surprised, I replied, 'Okay.' He led us inside the house, but just before we entered, he turns to us and briefed us again, 'Listen, the girl is the only family member here. She's only twelve years old. This is a foster home, and we haven't been able to contact the parents yet. She's sitting on the couch in the room.'

I felt my stomach being pushed up into my chest as if I was being punched in the guts. You could have struck me with a baseball bat, and I wouldn't have felt a thing. I immediately thought of my sister, who is two years younger than I am, and how she might have felt in this position.

As I walked into the room, I saw an obese woman sitting on one side of the room in an armchair. On the other side, a young girl is sitting by herself on a two-seater couch, crying uncontrollably. Any attempts to try and talk to her would have been futile, plus she was just twelve years of age. She's not going to remember anything I said or anyone else said to her at this time; her focus was her brother. We placed the card on the kitchen table.

The first thing I noticed in that room was that no one was comforting this innocent broken child, who was clearly at a loss in many ways. The large woman was just sitting there, showing no signs of distress, passively watching this young girl cry her eyes out. She was supposed to be the caregiver of this young girl who had been placed in her care.

In my head, I could only hear the drowning sound of my screams for someone to go over and be by her side. The feeling I got from the woman was far from concern, and she seemed unaffected by the events unfolding before her. It was heart-wrenching to watch this child mourn over the only resemblance of home and security she knew. I couldn't imagine myself at twelve years old being in a place I don't know, surrounded by strangers I don't know and losing the only family I had near me.

Watching the tears stream down her cheeks, like morning dew off a leaf, my thoughts of hopelessness quickly turned to anger at how two young children were left to fend for themselves because their parents were not fit to keep them.

To quote the Dalai Lama, 'Just as ripples spread out when a single pebble is dropped into water, the actions of individuals can have far-reaching effects.' Sometimes we don't know the true impact of our actions; this was a perfect example of precisely that.

Some couples spend thousands on trying to have children and create a family, and others have children and neglect them. There must be a feeling of injustice wash over the people listening to stories such as this.

I clearly remember walking out of that house with profound sadness. The usual conversation and small talk on the drive back to the city was replaced with a deafening silence. The only sounds I could hear were the sounds of the engine and the wheels rolling over the highway. I noticed small potholes and every bump as my mind raced away in deep reflection.

Finally, when the silence was broken, we exchanged our deepest sympathy for the girl and not once did we blame the boy for his actions. Not knowing the reasons for his drastic measures, we knew he was in a disadvantaged position with a world of responsibility on his shoulders. On top of that, he had a little sister to care for and protect. It was a massive responsibility to place on a child, one most adults would not be able to handle.

Every time I drive through the town of Rosebud, especially past that street, the visions and memories of that day flood my mind. I can still hear the echoes from that day. I wonder what came to be for that little girl: *Did that event of her childhood galvanise her into a better, stronger person?* I would hate to think a mist darker than night crept into her life as a side effect of her childhood.

One thing I took away from that day is that, in this world, there are some people striving to make it a better world for others, themselves and their children. Then there are others.

Tears in Heaven

*"The loss of a child
is my greatest nightmare."*
Angelina Jolie

Her love was like a beautiful rainbow, but gone too soon.

Sally left school early and decided to work at the local country club. They offered her full-time hours as she was responsible and organised. She was the perfect candidate. Sally always wanted to work in hospitality, and this was her chance.

One Friday night, she was serving a couple of guys named Clint and Andrew. Clint took an instant liking to Sally, and the flirting began to be exchanged back and forth. Clint knew Sally would be his wife and got her number that night.

After a few months, they were living together and couldn't be happier. They had the same dreams of one day starting a family together, and within five years, they were able to make that dream come true. By then, they had a three-year-old girl and a baby a few months old.

Finally, the life Sally had always imagined had come to fruition. She was the envy of her friends; she had a loving husband and two healthy children, and they were on the way to saving for a house for themselves.

As Clint worked long hours to support his young family, Sally would do what she could to keep up the household. On top of that, she would catch up with her mum twice a week. Sometimes, they would meet at the local shopping centre to browse the shops and talk about life. Other times, her mum would join them at a playground so the young girl could have a play. Sally relied on her mother for motherly advice and loved that her mother was a big part of her life and the lives of her children. Every so often, Sally would check in on her grandmother to make sure she was okay. She remembered as a kid how her grandmother always spoiled her. Now she could bring her children to her grandmother. Her grandmother loved the smiles and energy of the children. The grandmother always made sure she had treats on hand for when the three-year-old was coming to visit. The child would run as quickly as her little legs could carry her into her great grandmother's arms and eat as many treats as she could; it was like her own private Halloween every time.

One afternoon, Sally loaded the children into the car for a visit to her grandmother's house, unknown to her that this trip would change her life forever and for everyone around her.

This chapter, I would say, was the hardest to write by far. I wondered many times over and over if I should share this story. Eventually, I decided to include it. It is part of my experience. I will leave it to your discretion to skip this chapter if you choose, or continue to read on.

At the time that I was working as an undertaker, my wife and I were yet to have children. We had only recently married, and children were somewhere in our future plans. Now I have a daughter the same age as the beautiful little girl in the story below, who lived such a short life. My little girl is the cheekiest little girl you'll ever meet, but also witty and clever. I have boys older than she is, and she is the judge, jury and executioner to those three boys; they don't stand a chance against her.

When my daughter was about three years of age, and I was watching over her as she played, explored and tried to keep up with the boys, I was reminded of the young girl that day; how she would have been so full of beans with all the sensations of her new world. I had a sudden realisation that in this world you cannot always be there to protect the ones you love the most from the ugliness of the world – no matter how hard you try as a parent. I hate feeling defenceless. All I can do is love my children as much as I can and try to prepare them for the rest of their lives.

My life experiences have been somewhat different from the people in my circle of friends and family. My time as an undertaker has made me more protective of the people around me. In the Bible, I am reminded of Matthew 18:21-22, when Peter asked Jesus, 'Lord, how many times shall I forgive my brother? Shall I forgive him as many as seven times?'

Jesus replied, 'You must forgive him even if he does wrong to you 77 times.' Unfortunately, I've learnt the world isn't that forgiving.

On this particular day, everyone involved wished that this was a nightmare we could wake from.

THE SCENE

A text came through like an intruder breaking the mood. I had learnt to associate the sound of the text messages from my Nokia phone with sadness. It would resonate through my soul. The next thought that would come to mind was: *What are we about to encounter?*

Like a Manchurian Candidate, I looked at the phone and got dressed in a timely manner, ready for when the car arrived outside. As I glanced at my phone, I realised there was no address, just a street name and the cardinal direction of south. At first, I didn't know what this meant. When I got into the car, my partner explained that when we receive street names with no numbers, a suburb, and a cardinal reference, it generally means there has been a car accident, or someone has been struck by a vehicle.

By now, we anticipated that we were on our way to a car accident. The worst car accidents are usually late at night, when people have either been drinking, are affected by drugs, or are driving dangerously. If an accident is in the country late at night, we'll be driving for miles in the dark, guided by the car lights and the occasional street light dotted along the dark highways. When we roll over the horizon or around a bend, we would see a sea of flashing red, blue and white lights from the police cars and the ambulances illuminating the background. It's like watching fireworks in the night sky. I would always be in awe and mesmerised by the lights set on the darkened landscape. Knowing what awaited, however, took the joy out of the view pretty quickly.

In this case, the call came around 5 p.m. It was daylight savings time, so it was far from being dark. Being an afternoon accident, I wasn't sure what to expect. A thought was that it might have been a motorcycle rider who had come off their bike, like many others before. We pulled up to the accident, which already had the road closed signs in place. There wasn't a motorcycle in sight. Two smashed-up cars were a few feet from each other. The ground around both vehicles sparkled from the remnants of the broken windows, creating the illusion of a glittery floor on which the mangled wrecks of both cars sat. It didn't take an accident investigator to determine that it was a head-on crash.

The closer we got to one of the cars, where we could see the driver, now deceased, slumped over the steering wheel, a heavy scent of alcohol permeated the air like spilt drinks on the carpet of an old pub. The car was now looking more like a cheap convertible in a car sales yard with the roof removed to free the driver.

We pulled the stretcher out and placed it in the middle of the road to position it as close to the car as possible. The doors of the car could no longer open as the forceful impact had jammed them into the frame of the vehicle. We assessed the situation as to the best way to free this slouched man. We determine that going over the car door was not an option, given his larger than average body size. The only way this man was going to be removed from the car was through where the front window used to be.

My partner and I looked at each other to decide who was going to be the lucky one to jump onto the bonnet and pull this man free. I opted to give it a go as long as he was ready to catch me if I fell. The hood had a few flat spots to place my feet, but those flat spots were also very slippery with the shoes I was wearing. I jumped onto the hood of the car and gripped the man by the scruff of his shirt. I then pulled with all my might. A few officers and my partner were standing beside the car to help pull him over the dashboard of his car and onto the hood. With some difficulty and a team effort, we were able to free him from the carnage, place him on the stretcher and wheel him back to the van. And then load him in.

Thinking our job was completed and having a sense of accomplishment, I was surprised to hear an officer says, 'I'll take you to the second body.' Not having read the text thoroughly, my partner forgot to mention we were here for two deceased persons. Now knowing there was a second body, I unload the second stretcher, and ask, 'Where is the second body located?'

The police officer looked at my partner and me and then said in a quieter tone, 'Umm, you can kind-of leave the trolley here, the body is a three-year-old girl who's still in her child restraints.'

I couldn't believe what I had just heard. I *understood* every word the officer said, but I just couldn't believe it. My mind needed a moment to process the details. I was in a state of shock and disbelief.

'Ohh' was the only sound that escaped my lips. I felt I had been hit with a tonne of bricks that took all the wind out of me. We were led behind the other car. All I could see at first was a child restraint laying upside down on the road. Then, the horror of seeing two little legs, with the tiniest shoes still strapped to her feet, protruding from the chair broke my heart.

I was preparing myself for what we would see as we carefully turned the car seat over. It revealed a little girl strapped in her seat with both harness straps over her shoulders and clipped in securely, with barely a scratch on her. The only visible mark from the accident was a bruised forehead, which I presume she sustained when she struck the window after her chair broke free from the rear.

As my partner unbuckled her lifeless body, he picked her up. and carried her in his arms like a father carrying a sleeping child to the car after a late night. Her legs were dangling, and her arms were resting in his. We walked to the car like a funeral procession with heavy hearts.

The awaiting stretcher was covered in a clean white sheet and the unbuckled straps hung down on the sides. My partner ever so gently, like handling fine china, placed this tiny lifeless body in the middle of the oversized stretcher, as if not to wake her from her deep sleep. Instead of strapping her in as we had done immediately countless times before, his trembling hands slowly moved away from her and dropped by his side, like all the strength he had was gone – vanished into the late afternoon glow. As if we were mid-prayer in a cathedral, a blanket of silence fell over us. We were all frozen at the sight of this little girl. She still had the power she wielded upon us to pay her one last moment of silence. No one told us to do it; it was an unspoken moment of respect to this little girl who could be mistaken for sleeping.

After a few moments of silence, I started to notice the faint noises of the birds in the distance. I then felt every bit of the breeze, as it gently whirled around me like a fitted jacket. There were no other noises; no radios or phones or car engines running. As one of the police officers shook his head in disapproval, without muttering a word, I knew he wanted to voice his disgust along with some profanities. I think we all did that day. His gesture was enough; we just knew.

As the moment neared its end, my partner loaded the stretcher into the back of the van. The sound of the collapsing legs of the stretcher slapping against the back of the van broke the silence. It resembled the sound of prison doors shutting on a life sentence – her motionless body sliding inside with the stretcher.

There we stood in the middle of the carnage, surrounded by the panoramic views of vegetation and hills of the countryside. We stood paralysed and powerless. We knew at that moment a part of us would be locked away forever. We all lost a slice of our being with the little girl that day. *Never to return.*

The worst part of being a police officer, I would guess, would be breaking the news of a death to the family. I cannot think of a harder job. We all knew that there was a family out there whose life had changed forever.

As we returned to some form of normality, I asked one of the officers what had happened here. I wanted to understand what we had witnessed, and get some answers to make sense of, and attain some closure, on this tragedy.

The police officer responded. 'The guy you pulled out by the scruff of his shirt earlier, was in one of the cars, driving alone. He was unlicensed, drunk and the car is unregistered. As he pulled around this high-crowned road, he lost control of the car and smashed into an oncoming car, which was travelling on the opposite side of the road.' He pointed to the corner and then the cars as he spoke. 'The oncoming car was being driven by a young mother, with a young baby and the three-year-old girl in child restraints in the back. They are the victims of this careless, irresponsible individual.'

I clearly remember all the hairs on the back of my neck began to rise as my body ignited with anger. A horrifying feeling of disgust crept inside me until it took over every part of my body. Knowing that this deplorable, selfish individual had escaped justice in death and that he would never understand the gravity of his actions and the impact on so many people, was sickening.

That day, he robbed so many people of so much. He robbed the life of a beautiful girl, and the world of all the smiles she would have shared. He robbed the family of an angel, and a mother and father of a daughter. If he were alive, I would not care if he spent the rest of his natural life in a prison cell, reminiscing how much his selfish actions had impacted everyone.

When I got home that night, I couldn't bring myself to share what I had witnessed with my wife. This was personal, and I felt my core shaken. A few days later, I told my wife what had happened; she was devastated.

Having experienced this, I have always made sure my children are correctly restrained every time, as the horrible memory of that sight looms as a constant reminder.

Even though it has been years now, as a general fighting the last war even long after the final gun falls silent, the image of that day comes back to haunt me now and again. I know that day is now part of me and will continue to haunt me like a homing pigeon finding its way home. I've learnt to live with most memories I still carry.

I completely understand and appreciate why men and women find it hard to bring themselves to share their stories of war or other traumatic events. People, I have learnt, cope differently to situations. Some cope better than others, and others are crippled by the events.

Living with the Dead

*"Dead people have a right
to be heard and seen."*
ANTHONY T. HINCKS

Anish worked in a hospital cleaning surgical tools for various hospitals. He loved his job because there wasn't much to think about. His colleagues considered him 'the social butterfly', although he wasn't always the easiest person to work with. He was outspoken, always wanting people to value his views, and had a basic disregard for others. Even though he came out as a gay man five years earlier, he lived a double life when it came to his parents. He never dared to tell them he was gay. He grew up in a strict Indian family, and his parents hoped he would get married and have children of his own.

Anish tried to hide his other life from his parents by living overseas. He felt this was the best option, thinking if they knew, he would bring dishonour to his family. This was a demon that he fought with for years. He would always seek comfort from his circle of friends.

One day, Anish's boss, Susan, called him into her office and informed him that he was to go to a neighbouring hospital for a couple of days to train some of the recruits. Anish saw this as an opportunity to impress his boss – a chance to show her that he was willing to take on more responsibility and prove himself.

On arrival at the new hospital, Anish meets Matt, a full-time nurse. Matt immediately took away any breath Anish had. His heart skipped a beat and his knees went weak. Anish had to take in a couple of deep breaths to recompose himself.

Matt was a confident, younger man with chiselled features. Anish knew straight away that Matt was also gay. For most of the first day, Anish took every opportunity to bump into Matt. By the second morning, Anish had managed to get Matt's interest and ask him out to lunch. Lunch turned into dinner, and dinner turned into a sleepover. Before long, Anish and Matt were living together.

With Matt's hectic working hours, trying to do as much overtime as possible, Anish mainly watched TV and worked casually when they needed him. After a while, Anish lost his job as new machinery replaced his role. With Matt supporting him, Anish did not seek out a new job. Instead, he did all the housework and cooked the meals for Matt and himself. Some nights, Anish would stay up all night watching TV and then sleep through the morning. This became Matt and Anish's new normal, and they were both happy – for a while.

Anish's life soon revolved around the television and he stacked on more weight. He lost all motivation to leave the house, even to buy groceries. Matt got used to seeing Anish asleep in front of the TV. If Anish was asleep in the chair when he woke up, Matt would pack his lunch for work and head off, trying not to wake Anish up.

One night, Anish fell asleep in front of the TV in his robe for the last time. The next morning, Matt headed off to work.

THE SCENE

We pulled up to an address around mid-afternoon. Curious kids were riding their bicycles up and down the street. This reminded me of my childhood; how we use to ride around finding things to do and games to play.

As we opened the car doors, the distinctive smell of decomposing flesh filled the air and flew through our nostrils. It's a smell we knew well. At this house, it was a heavy and thick pungent smell which seemed to cling to the fabric of our suits.

We walked to the front door that was already open, presumably to let fresh air in, and were greeted by the police officers already standing inside. They told us that the body had been there for a week, before they led us down the hallway to the kitchen. The smells progressively became more and more unbearable.

I think everyone has one part of their job they try to avoid or hate. My pet hate would have to be the smell of rotting flesh. No matter how often I came across the same scent, I never got used to it. It was an unavoidable part of the job, and there was no escaping. Most of the time, the best defence was to hold my breath, zip up the body bag as quickly as possible and run out to inhale fresh air, like a free diver coming up for air. This always reminded me of a game we played as kids to see how long we could hold our breath underwater.

As soon as the paperwork was filled out, I dreaded what was to come next. Another police officer led us to the living room where a deceased, overweight man larger than life was sitting in an old recliner facing the TV. He was cloaked in a dressing gown, his chin deep in his neck. As we got closer, more details of the man became visible: his stale blood-filled arms, his legs like tree trunks, the veins in his arms and legs looking ready to burst, like overfilled water balloons. I walked around to the front of the couch and the sheer size of the man became apparent. I knew this was going to be a task in itself.

Unsuccessfully, we attempted to pull his shoulders off the couch. As we tried to move the man forward by pulling his robe, the couch came along with it. The blood had permeated and seeped through his skin and his clothes and then dried. Now, the couch and the man were fused. This man's back was cemented to the backrest of the armchair.

After some consideration, we decided that the only option was to place the body bag directly in front of the couch below the man's feet and slide him straight into the bag from the sofa. This way each person could grip a side.

The plan was sound, and we had the manpower ready. Unfortunately, executing the plan was entirely different altogether! We each grabbed hold of the man and began to pull him away from the chair. As we pulled, his feet stopped him from moving, acting like two sturdy support beams. Constantly reassessing, I decided to grip between his calf muscles and ankles to free his feet. As I did this, I could feel the grit of the dried blood through his skin on my millimetre-thin gloves I was wearing. It reminded me of a deceased lady that was in the bath for a week – when we pulled her out by the arms, her skin separated from her muscles like surgical gloves. I was trying not to do the same with this guy, but his skin felt like it would come off if I pulled too hard.

I changed the force of my grip and began to hold his feet tighter to lift them off the ground and into the bag, rather than the initial sliding motion we were attempting. As I did so, my fingers ruptured his skin, creating a hole. This allowed his bodily fluids to drain, which then cascaded from the hole to swiftly engulf my hands. Even though I was wearing gloves, the sensation was intolerably unbearable as I felt the icy cold fluid swoop over the back of my hands like one-hundred tiny spiders.

Having no time to think, his body suddenly launched into momentum. We manoeuvred him into the middle of the body bag like an emergency landing of a Boeing 747 filled with passengers. After the deceased came to rest into this position, we looked up and glared at his permanent silhouette of blood on the couch where he had sat for days.

We zipped him up and, with great difficulty given his sheer weight, moved his body over to the stretcher inch by inch. He was the heaviest man I had encounter thus far. We had to enlist the help of the attending police officers to help lift the stretcher and lock the wheels in the upright position. Like a full shopping trolley through a crowded car park, we struggled to manoeuvre the trolley to the awaiting van.

When we went back inside, we found out more details of what had happened. One of the police officers elaborated on the situation and how this man's large body was discovered.

We found out that his male partner worked as a nurse in the health industry. The nature of his work meant he was gone from the house for many hours, day and night, and on odd days. Regularly, he worked double shifts. The deceased man did not work and spent most of his time watching TV. He spent long hours in front of the TV for the best part of the day and night. Many times before, he'd fallen asleep while watching TV.

After the man had died, his partner would walk past the living area, glance over at the man and think he was asleep and therefore, went about his normal routine. This continued for almost a week before his partner had the realisation that his partner may not be sleeping. He went to check on him, and it became obvious that he'd been dead for some time. That's when he raised the alarm.

The odd thing about the whole ordeal was that when we pulled up in the driveway and disembarked from the car, we knew immediately that there was a dead person inside who had been there for some time because of the smell. We wondered why the man's partner and the neighbours had not realised the same thing. I was sure the smell would be a dead giveaway that something wasn't right.

On the drive away, with the dead man on the stretcher in the back of the van, we had all windows down to let the smell out. I still kept wondering why no one had noticed the offensive odour. A little while later, I looked into it; I wanted an explanation.

Here is what I learnt: When a frog is placed in a pot of boiling water, it becomes uncomfortable promptly. It notices the danger and hops out. Remarkably, when the frog is placed in cold water, and the heat is gradually increasing, the frog continually regulates its body temperature and adjusts it to its new surroundings. It does not notice the danger until it's too late.

Our odour receptors in our nasal cavity work similarly. The triggers to offensive smells, such as rotten fruit and dangerous food and gases, that have served us for millions of years, send signals to the olfactory bulb in the brain's limbic system, which in turn instructs us as to what we are smelling, and whether it's pleasurable, offensive or dangerous. It also helps us create memories by attaching a sense of smell to an event, such as the smell of freshly cut grass triggering a memory of playing in the yard as a child.

After approximately three minutes, the receptors begin to experience temporary sensory fatigue, also known as olfactory adaptation. This results in the receptors beginning to stop sending messages to the brain as they are exhausted due to prolong exposure. In short, this is also known as nose blindness, which is when you begin to focus on new smells.

In this case, when the man died, many of the neighbours could smell something in the first place, but after three minutes of exposure, their nasal cavity began to focus on new smells, and this was how he went unnoticed for so long.

Red Red Wine

*"First you take a drink, then the drink
takes a drink, then the drink takes you."*
F. Scott Fitzgerald

Garry, oh, Garry. Never able to find a woman in his life to stay around long enough to marry him. Garry was a man in his fifties. As he had grown older, it became harder and harder to find a soulmate. After working at a bank for 35 years, he received a redundancy – his services were no longer required. Realising he didn't have much to retire on, Garry decided to get a job at an electrical appliance store. There he was given the tasks of bookkeeping and payroll. He had a little office set off to the side, and before long, found himself embedded at the shop like old furniture. Not having a wife or kids, Garry turned to the bottle for reassurance and comfort. He'd been a drinker most of his life, but as time went by, his drinking became more and more frequent. It got to a stage where he would bring a bottle to work to have a drink with his lunch. Soon his drinking habit got the best of him. Sometimes, he would bring two bottles to work as one no longer seemed enough.

Every lunchtime, Garry headed to his car after a cigarette. He ate his sandwich and washed it down with a bottle of red. It became apparent among his colleagues that Garry was drinking on the job. They decided to report him to the director of the business, Marty. Marty would excuse Garry's actions or brush off the accusations.

He would sternly say, 'If I see him with a bottle, I'll fire him! But what he does in his car is his business.'

This was more of a coded message that Garry does his work well, and the business relied on him. Marty gave the vibe that he wanted everyone to keep quiet about Garry's drinking and never bring it up again, like the uncle no one talks about in the family.

Being a young director with little experience, Marty didn't think Garry's drinking would affect the business as long as Garry stayed away from the customers and did his job. No one said anything to Garry, so Garry saw this as a pass to keep doing what he was doing. Garry loved his job and the perks.

Then came the day when Garry opened his computer to find an email saying, "Congratulations! You've won first prize of a year's supply of wine." Garry had entered a competition about six weeks earlier, which required him to rate different types of wines produced in the area. Now, with first prize, he would have the opportunity to sample wines from the local wineries. Garry rang the number, and sure enough, it was real. He gave them directions for delivery to his house. A few nights later, Garry arrived home from work to find the delivery of the first month's supply of wines sitting on his front doorstep. There were two crates of wine to sample, and this would happen every month for the next 12 months.

For Garry, this was equivalent to winning the lottery. On that first night, he drank up nearly a whole crate while watching TV. The next morning, feeling heady, he called in sick. Unable to hold back, he spent the entire day drinking again. *It was like a love affair between two people.*

The third month passed. Garry's drinking had taken over his life more than ever. He was taking days off work to fuel his love affair. By now, his productivity at work had dropped dramatically, and Marty had to pull him aside a couple of times to have a chat to Garry to try and get him back on track. Assuring Marty that there's nothing wrong, Garry continues his work.

Then, one morning Garry doesn't show up for work. Marty put it down to Garry's late-night binge drinking. He assumed Garry was sleeping it off. The next morning, Garry again did not come in, and there was no phone call from Garry as to the reason for his absence. By lunchtime, Marty was so concerned that he rang the local police station and explained the situation. The police officer told him that they will check on Garry's whereabouts. A few hours later, Marty received a phone call confirming his worst fears.

THE SCENE

Even just thinking about writing this chapter makes me want to throw up. I can still taste that thick revolting smell, which permeated the air in that room on that particular afternoon.

We rolled through the afternoon traffic and casually pulled up to the address. Usually, when we arrive at a house, there is one or maybe two police cars, but this time we were spellbound to find what looked like a parking lot of police cars. From crime scene investigators and detectives, to the attending police officers, everyone was there. For some reason though, it seemed more casual than usual; police were walking in and out of the house like a Christmas party was happening inside. I expected to hear music blaring as I opened my car door.

We strolled up to the front door. All the curtains and windows of the house were open, so we knew this body was going to smell. How bad was anyone's guess. But little did we know that things were going to get worse — *a lot worse.*

As we made our way to the kitchen, we walked past a wall of empty wine bottles stacked neatly one on top of another. The display was about waist height and stretched the length of the front entrance. There were well over 100 bottles here, easily, I guessed.

We jokingly commented that this guy loved his wine, but we were about to find out firsthand how much wine. Most attending police had gathered in the kitchen area. One of the officers said that the deceased man was in a wine club and had a drinking problem. This was evident given the amount of wine he had stacked up.

After we'd completed the formalities, our real work began. One of the officers led us through to the living room. The man we were here to collect was sitting on an old three-seater sofa. His head was leaning as far back as it could over the headrest, with his neck exposed and stretched out. His bottom jaw, weighed down by gravity, revealed stained teeth in his wide-open mouth. His arms rested by his sides in a relaxed position where they came to rest. The only sound missing from the scene was a deep rumbling snore, and you would think he was asleep. Assessing the body and its position, I thought to myself, "Yep! This is going to be an easy job! No decomposed body, no mess. Beautiful!" *Boy, was I horribly wrong!*

As we grabbed him by his arms to pull him into an upright position, the motion flung his head forward and, like a well-designed catapult from the medieval ages, an avalanche of vomit mixed with the gastric-acid juices from inside his stomach and stale blood came rushing out through his mouth like Niagara Falls and covered his chest and the surrounding area. This was followed by a strong, pungent gastric odour mixed in with the two-day-old vomit …

In less than a second, everyone that could make a quick escape made a mad rush for fresh air. People standing near windows had half their bodies hanging out, revealing a sea of faces turning all different colours:

from green to red and pale white. Others, including myself, managed to get outside. Some were affected more than others and started dry retching. I thought it was only a matter of time before someone was going to throw up. I felt the back of my mouth water up and spew beginning to make its way up, but nothing came up as I too dry retched. It was at that moment that I started to weigh up the pros and cons of my paycheque for the work I was doing. Moments like this made me question the direction my life was taking; whether I'd made the right choices or not. If the sight of decomposing bodies and mixed cocktails in different colours of vomit didn't turn you off, the smell was the knock-out.

Because the man was a heavy drinker for years and was drunk, at some point, he had drowned on his own vomit while suffering a brain haemorrhage. His head was tilted back, which prevented everything from coming out. Whatever he ate earlier added to the cocktail of horror. It was like the perfect storm had collided in sync to merge and create a symphony.

I clearly remember not wanting to re-enter the room. The windows that were fully open were not nearly enough to clear the air. We had to hold our breath again to complete this job. By this stage, my lungs had developed into deep-sea diver's lungs, but still, this wasn't enough. We had to exit the room multiple times just to surface for some fresh air, before going back in with our breath held.

After a short while, we managed to get him into the van. This was worse than any decomposing body. I hate the smell of vomit. If I see anyone else vomit, I start dry retching and sometimes vomit. It was only luck that I didn't in this case. I certainly didn't want the police officers to see me vomit. Given that I did this on a daily basis, you'd think I would be used to it. The windows of the van couldn't go any lower on our drive away. It made me question why car manufacturers didn't make bigger windows. Being stuck in a car with the putrid smell of vomit made me feel sick for the rest of the day.

***

Not long after this job, I knew my adventure was nearing its end. I couldn't bear to experience another case like this or any others from before. I had hit my limit. I knew I'd had enough. It had been approximately two years since I had started. I'd learnt so much in a relatively short period of time and I now saw the world from a completely different perspective.

I remember thinking about what I would do next. What skills had I acquired from this job which I could take on a new path, a new direction? I didn't feel I had many skills behind me, and that made me worried about my future. I had to develop other skills if I wanted to get to the level I imagined myself to be at. Even with these doubts, it wasn't long before I decided to hand in my resignation.

Whatever my calling was, I knew this wasn't it. Like a prisoner contemplating his escape, I wondered what I was going to do, who I wanted to be. And I was willing to do what it took to get there – I had discovered what my new limits were and how far I was ready to go. Sometimes, you need to experience what you don't want in order to have some clarity of what you really want to accomplish.

In Closing

*"We are all in the gutter but
some of us are looking at the stars."*
Oscar Wilde

I was privileged to experience something that most people would have no idea about. Sharing my experiences with you of a world cloaked in mystery and intrigue is a privilege in itself. Two questions I would often be asked: how did I feel about my experience? And did I have any religious experiences on the job?

I will address the questions in order.

How did I feel about my experience? To sum it up quickly and easily, it was like any other job most of the time. For the most part, I recognised that I was lucky enough to experience what most people never would. It shed some light on what we humans are capable of and how fragile life can be. However, I wouldn't be human if I didn't feel touched and saddened by the stories, events and sights I have witnessed. I hope I have imparted these feelings to you. I have learnt not to assume how people will respond to death. Some people look like a rock, only to crumble into a ball of dust. Others who you wouldn't expect to be strong, turn out to be the rock for everyone around them. And then there is everyone in between.

I would be lying if I said I didn't feel like a ball of dust at some points, and there were moments where I thought I'd crumble, but from somewhere I found courage. All up, I would say my time as an undertaker was a humbling experience. I realised as humans, we all have our limits; *we are all breakable.*

Now, to address the second question. To talk about my religious experiences and beliefs is always hard, without offending anyone's views. I have thought a lot about what I was going to write. I knew what I wanted to say, but I have had to find the proper context in which to express my views.

I grew up in a Catholic household. I even served as an altar boy for several years. As a child, having faith was a mantra my family adopted. This wasn't enough for me. I joined bible study groups and had discussions with a number of people about faith and religion. As I got older, my ever-thinking mind began to rationalise my beliefs, and there was a time where I struggled to place them within the real world. Somewhere along my journey, I stumbled on a philosophical argument called 'Pascal's wager', presented in the seventeenth century by Blaise Pascal. It has since been the forefront of religious debate. This notion was known for years before Pascal first put it into context.

No matter what you invest your belief in; whether it be Catholicism, Judaism, Islamic, Buddhism, Zoroastrianism, Falun Gong, or the many other belief systems out there, the end goal is to go to a heavenly destination, as opposed to that 'Hell' we all learn to steer away from. And, it is assumed we will get to Heaven by practising what we are taught in our religious circles.

There are stories of people who say they "saw the light" in near-death experiences, but no one has been to the afterworld and come back to tell us about it, other than in textbooks dated thousands of years ago. No one can physically measure the afterworld by any means; no telescope is strong enough, no tape measure long enough, or scales big enough. We are left to trust our belief. Blaise Pascal saw this as an issue, so he posed the question: *Is it better for us mere mortals to believe in God, or live our lives as good people and not to believe in God?*

Now, Pascal was also a mathematician who co-founded the study of probability. So, his argument rested on chance and outcomes. There are only four outcomes to the question posed by Pascal:

If you believe in God, and there is a heaven.

1. You get to go to Heaven if you believe.

2. You are condemned to Hell for eternity if you don't believe.

Now, let's say you live a reasonably good life or not but don't believe in God.

3. You don't go to Heaven because there is no Heaven.

4. You don't go to Hell because there is no Hell.

The obvious answer here for those who believe in God is option one: you believe and the ultimate prize is to go to Heaven. The rationale is that the risk outweighs the reward, so it's better to be safe than sorry. By choosing to believe, Heaven is the reward. No one wants to spend an eternity in Hell, given the option.

This is where Pascal's wager gets interesting. In short, if gods are omnipotent, which is the quality of being almighty and having unlimited power, they would also have the ability to be everywhere at once. This would arguably be the main attribute of all gods, as most religious belief systems tend to agree.

But, would God allow a believer, who has sinned just as much as a non-believer, to enter Heaven for merely placing his belief in a spiritual body – without a shred of evidence – for none other than an insurance policy? Would God be fallible? This would surely go against being omnipotent.

In other words, if God does exist, there is no hiding from God if God holds all the attributes of being omnipotent. He would see through to our darkest, deepest secrets and see only why we believed in the first place; an insurance policy.

I always wondered how some could genuinely believe in something to be true if it cannot be measured by any means. Remember, this is only my view; I don't speak for anyone else. Another main reason I choose to believe is that we live, we die and we are part of the great circle of life that happens biologically. If you take all the factors that make us human beings, such as copper, zinc, iron, and so on, we are all constructed from mere stardust.

Through my experiences, one thing I have come to understand and accept is that there are, four noble truths. These are the essence of Buddhism – that life is suffering. They teach us that life has invisible suffering, and there is a cause of our suffering. Also, there is an end to our suffering, and the path to the end of suffering. We all would love to live in a utopian world, but you cannot escape the four noble truths. No matter how much we try to escape pain, it will always exist in our life. We can only try and live as good people and do good in the world.

I would like to thank you for giving me the privilege of sharing my stories with you. I hope this has shed some light on an occupation that is mostly unknown to the average person, yet will cross paths with nearly everyone at some point. Thank you for allowing me to take you on a journey into this part of my life. I hope it has been an experience like no other. My time spent writing these has brought back different emotions, and at times, I have struggled to find the words to express the events, thoughts and context. At times, it has been difficult to share these experiences as I have had to relive the scenes, senses, thoughts and emotions. Some memories made me laugh while I remembered the good times, and others brought me to the verge of tears from profound sadness. I had to recall just how unfair life had been for some people.

This is my first book and I look forward to writing about more experiences in the future and sharing these stories with you.

www.ingramcontent.com/pod-product-compliance
Lightning Source LLC
Chambersburg PA
CBHW031324060726
47590CB00003B/1326